PRENTICE HALL

UNITED STATES HISTORY

All-in-One Teaching Resources

An Era of Protest and Change (1960–1980)

PEARSON
Prentice Hall

Upper Saddle River, New Jersey
Boston, Massachusetts

Acknowledgements

Page 17: Source: Silent Spring by Rachel Carson
Page 17: Source: The New York Times, July 22, 1962
Page 19: ALICE'S RESTAURANT by Arlo Guthrie. Copyright © 1966 (renewed) by APPLESEED MUSIC, INC. All rights reserved. Used by permission

NOTE: Every effort has been made to locate the copyright owner of material reprinted in this book. Omissions brought to our attention will be corrected in subsequent editions.

Upper Saddle River, New Jersey
Boston, Massachusetts

ISBN 0-13-203706-8

1 2 3 4 5 6 7 8 9 10 10 09 08 07 06

BD

* The Issues Connector worksheet may be modified for students as follows:

L1 Ask students to read one of the excerpts. Review any vocabulary that may cause difficulty in comprehension. Then, have students rewrite the excerpt in their own words. During class discussion, call on these students first to share their work.

L2 Have students read one of the excerpts and the corresponding background note. Have them identify any difficult vocabulary, and review definitions with them. Then, have students summarize the selection in a short paragraph and explain the context in which it was written.

L3 Give students the background notes and primary sources. Have them complete the worksheet.

L4 Give students the background notes and primary sources. Have them complete the worksheet. As an extension, ask students to conduct a debate based on the question asked on the feature in the textbook. As an alternate activity, have students find current events articles that relate to the issue involved. Ask them to compare the articles to the excerpts given and explain their own position on the issue.

Name _____ Class _____ Date _____

Letter Home

Dear Family,

Over the coming weeks, our United States history class will be reading a chapter called An Era of Protest and Change. The following information will give you some background to the content your student will be studying.

Following the relative calm of the 1950s, American culture experienced numerous changes during the 1960s and 1970s. The Vietnam War and the civil rights movement spawned a counterculture movement that opposed the materialism and conformity that prevailed during the 1950s. A generation gap emerged, as evidenced by everything from political views to clothing to music. In response to the civil rights movement, women renewed their pursuit of equal rights and challenged society's traditional views of women. American women sought to distance themselves from housewife stereotypes that were prevalent during the 1950s and early 1960s. After writing *The Feminine Mystique,* Betty Friedan helped to establish the National Organization for Women (NOW) that solidified the women's movement. NOW worked to pass the Equal Rights Amendment, but some feminists felt that the organization was either too radical or too tame. Despite this division, women made important gains regarding working conditions and birth control.

Other groups also struggled for equal rights during the 1960s and 1970s. Mexican Americans worked as migrant workers on the West Coast for decades and suffered under exploitative immigration regulations. In 1962, Cesar Chavez organized a farmworkers' union in California to demand fair treatment and wages. The Chicano movement, which sought broader equal rights for Mexican Americans, also developed during this time. Native Americans embraced the spirit of the civil rights movement and organized the American Indian Movement to work for self-determination on Native American lands. In the early 1970s, Native Americans staged demonstrations in Washington, D.C., and at Wounded Knee, site of the 1890 massacre of Sioux in South Dakota. Rights for consumers and the disabled also were strengthened during this period.

One of the biggest changes in American life during the 1960s and 1970s was increased government commitment to the environment. Following the publication of *Silent Spring* by Rachel Carson in 1962, Americans became more aware of the harm done by industry to the environment. President Nixon and Congress worked to pass legislation, such as the Clean Air Act and the Endangered Species Act, that would improve environmental conditions. Although the government sought to raise environmental awareness, incidents at Love Canal, New York, and at Three Mile Island outside of Harrisburg, Pennsylvania, indicated that many changes were still needed to protect the environment.

In the weeks ahead, your student may wish to share what he or she is learning with you. Please participate in your child's educational experience through discussion and involvement.

Sincerely,

UNA ERA DE PROTESTAS Y CAMBIO
Carta para el hogar

Estimada familia,

En las próximas semanas, nuestra clase de historia de Estados Unidos va a leer un capítulo llamado Una Era de Protestas y Cambio. La siguiente información le dará a usted algunos conocimientos sobre el tema que su estudiante va a estudiar.

La cultura estadounidense experimentó numerosos cambios durante las décadas de 1960 y 1970. La Guerra de Vietnam y el movimiento por los derechos civiles engendró un movimiento de contracultura que se oponía al materialismo y el conformismo que prevalecía durante la década de 1950. Se produjo un lapso generacional, como se evidencia en todo, desde los puntos de vista políticos hasta la ropa y la música. En respuesta al movimiento por los derechos civiles, las mujeres renovaron su búsqueda por la igualdad de derechos y enjuiciaron la visión tradicional de las mujeres. Las mujeres estadounidenses querían distanciarse de los estereotipos de dueñas de casa que prevalecieron durante la década de 1950 y comienzos de la década de 1960. Luego de escribir *The Feminine Mystique (La mística femenina)*, Betty Friedman ayudó a establecer Organización Nacional para las Mujeres (NOW, por sus siglas en inglés) que daba solidez al movimiento de las mujeres. NOW trabajó para que se aprobara la enmienda por la igualdad de derechos, pero algunas feministas pensaban que la organización era muy radical o muy dócil.

Otros grupos también lucharon por la igualdad de derechos durante las décadas de 1960 y 1970. Los mexicano-estadounidenses trabajaban como obreros inmigrantes en la costa oeste durante décadas y sufrían bajo las reglamentaciones explotadoras de inmigración. En 1962, César Chavez organizó un sindicato de obreros de las granjas en California para protestar por un trato y salarios justos. El movimiento chicano, que buscaba mayor igualdad de derechos para los mexicano-estadounidenses, también se desarrolló durante esta época. Los indígenas americanos adoptaron el espíritu del movimiento por los derechos civiles y organizaron el Movimiento Indio Estadounidense, para trabajar por la autodeterminación en tierra de indígenas americanos. A principios de la década de 1970, los indígenas americanos realizaron demostraciones en Washington, D.C., y en Wounded Knee. Los derechos de los consumidores y de los discapacitados también mejoraron durante este período.

Uno de los mayores cambios en la vida estadounidense durante las décadas de 1960 y 1970 fue un mayor compromiso por parte del gobierno con respecto al medio ambiente. Luego de la publicación de *Silent Spring (Primavera silenciosa)* de Rachel Carson en 1962, los estadounidenses fueron más concientes de los daños causados por la industria al medio ambiente. El presidente Nixon y el congreso trabajaron para aprobar legislaciones como la Ley del aire limpio y la Ley de las especies en peligro de extinción, que mejoraran las condiciones ambientales. Aunque el gobierno buscaba aumentar la conciencia sobre el medio ambiente, los incidentes en Love Canal, Nueva York y en Three Mile Island a las afueras de Harrisburg, Pennsylvania indicaban que todavía se necesitaban muchas mejoras para proteger el medio ambiente.

En las próximas semanas, es posible que su estudiante quiera compartir con usted lo que ha aprendido. Por favor participe en la experiencia educativa de su hijo o hija a través de conversaciones e involucrándose en su trabajo.

Atentamente,

AN ERA OF PROTEST AND CHANGE 1960–1980

1. The Counterculture

Pacing
2 periods
1 block

L1	Special Needs
L2	Basic to Average
L3	All Students
L4	Average to Advanced

Section Objectives

- Describe the rise of the counterculture.
- List the major characteristics of the counterculture.
- Evaluate the impact of the counterculture on American values and society.

Terms and People • counterculture • generation gap • Beatles • commune • Haight-Ashbury • Timothy Leary

Focus Question: What was the counterculture, and what impact did it have on American society?

PREPARE TO READ

Build Background Knowledge
Preview the section, and have students discuss the outcomes of the civil rights movement.

Set a Purpose
Have students discuss the Witness History Selection. Point out the Section Focus Question, and have students fill in the Note Taking graphic organizer.

Preview Key Terms
Preview the section's Key Terms.

Instructional Resources
❑ **WITNESS HISTORY** Audio CD
❑ **All in One** **Teaching Resources**
   L3 Preread the Chapter, p. 8
   L3 Analyze Visuals, p. 10
   L3 Vocabulary Builder, p. 11
❑ **Reading and Note Taking Study Guide**
   (On-Level, Adapted, and Spanish)
   Section 1

TEACH

The Counterculture Rises
Describe the roots and values of the 1960s counterculture.

Defining the Counterculture
Discuss how music, art, spirituality, and sexual behavior defined the counterculture.

The Counterculture Ends
Explain the causes behind people's disillusionment with the counterculture.

Instructional Resources
❑ **All in One** **Teaching Resources**
   L3 Link to Literature: "Alice's Restaurant," p. 19
❑ **Color Transparencies**
   L3 Changing Fashions, p. 71
❑ **Note Taking Transparencies,** B-138

ASSESS/RETEACH

Assess Progress
Evaluate student comprehension with the Section Assessment and Section Quiz.

Reteach
Assign the Reading and Note Taking Study Guide to help struggling students.

Extend
Have students research important events from 1969 to create a time capsule.

Instructional Resources
❑ **All in One** **Teaching Resources**
   L4 Enrichment: Time Capsule, p. 13
   L3 Section Quiz, p. 24
❑ **Reading and Note Taking Study Guide**
   (On-Level, Adapted, and Spanish)
   Section 1 Summary
❑ **Progress Monitoring Transparencies,** 134

Audio support is available for this section.
Modify lesson with notes found on the bottom of the Teacher's Edition.

AN ERA OF PROTEST AND CHANGE 1960–1980

2. The Women's Rights Movement

Pacing
2 periods
1 block

L1	Special Needs
L2	Basic to Average
L3	All Students
L4	Average to Advanced

Section Objectives

■ Analyze how a movement for women's rights arose in the 1960s.

■ Explain the goals and tactics of the women's movement.

■ Assess the impact of the women's movement on American society.

Terms and People • feminism • Betty Friedan • NOW • ERA • Gloria Steinem • Phyllis Schlafly • *Roe* v. *Wade*

Focus Question: What led to the rise of the women's movement, and what impact did it have on American society?

PREPARE TO READ

Build Background Knowledge
Preview the section, and remind students that women won the right to vote in 1920 after a long struggle.

Set a Purpose
Have students discuss the Witness History Selection. Point out the Section Focus Question, and have students fill in the Note Taking graphic organizer.

Preview Key Terms
Preview the section's Key Terms.

Instructional Resources
❏ **WITNESS HISTORY** Audio CD

❏ **All in One Teaching Resources**
   L3 Reading Strategy, p. 12
❏ **Reading and Note Taking Study Guide**
   (On-Level, Adapted, and Spanish)
   Section 2

TEACH

A Women's Movement Arises
Explain how the civil rights movement and the search for better jobs led to a rise in feminism.

Women Find Their Voices
Explore the tactics of NOW and the opinions of its opponents.

Lasting Effects of the Women's Movement
Discuss the legal and social changes brought about by the women's movement.

Instructional Resources
❏ **All in One Teaching Resources**
   L1 L2 Biography: Gloria Steinem, p. 20
   L3 Biography: Women's Rights Activists, p. 21
❏ **Color Transparencies**
   L3 The Equal Rights Amendment, p. 72
❏ **Note Taking Transparencies,** B-139

ASSESS/RETEACH

Assess Progress
Evaluate student comprehension with the Section Assessment and Section Quiz.

Reteach
Assign the Reading and Note Taking Study Guide to help struggling students.

Extend
Have students make illustrated charts showing feminism's social, political, and economic impact on the United States.

Instructional Resources
❏ **All in One Teaching Resources**
   L3 Section Quiz, p. 25
❏ **Reading and Note Taking Study Guide**
   (On-Level, Adapted, and Spanish)
   Section 2 Summary
❏ **Progress Monitoring Transparencies,** 135

Audio support is available for this section.
Modify lesson with notes found on the bottom of the Teacher's Edition.

Name _____ Class _____ Date _____ M T W T F

AN ERA OF PROTEST AND CHANGE 1960–1980

3. The Rights Revolution Expands

Pacing
2 periods
1 block

L1	Special Needs
L2	Basic to Average
L3	All Students
L4	Average to Advanced

Section Objectives

- Explain how the Latino population grew after World War I.
- Analyze the Latino and Native American rights movements of the 1960s and 1970s.
- Describe the expansion of rights for consumers and the disabled.

Terms and People • Cesar Chavez • migrant farmworker • UFW • Chicano movement • AIM • Ralph Nader

Focus Question: How did the rights movements of the 1960s and 1970s expand rights for diverse groups of Americans?

PREPARE TO READ

Build Background Knowledge
Preview the section, and recall the goals and tactics of the earlier civil rights movement.

Set a Purpose
Have students discuss the Witness History Selection. Point out the Section Focus Question, and have students fill in the Note Taking graphic organizer.

Preview Key Terms
Preview the section's Key Terms.

Instructional Resources
❏ **WITNESS HISTORY** Audio CD
❏ **Reading and Note Taking Study Guide**
(On-Level, Adapted, and Spanish)
Section 3

TEACH

The Latino Population Grows
Explain the factors that led to increased Latino immigration.

Pressing for Equal Rights
Discuss how different groups struggled for rights and recognition.

Native Americans Push for Equality
Explore how Native American activist groups formed and confronted the government.

New Rights for Consumers and the Disabled
Describe the growth of consumer advocacy groups and the gains made by people with disabilities.

Instructional Resources
❏ **All in One Teaching Resources**
  L3 History Comics: Cesar Chavez and the UFW, p. 22
❏ **Skills Handbook**
  L3 Evaluate Understanding, p. 16
❏ **Color Transparencies**
  L3 The Latino Movement, p. 73
❏ **Note Taking Transparencies,** B-140a, B-140b

ASSESS/RETEACH

Assess Progress
Evaluate student comprehension with the Section Assessment and Section Quiz.

Reteach
Assign the Reading and Note Taking Study Guide to help struggling students.

Extend
Have students write an analysis comparing one protest movement not covered in the textbook to the other movements about which they have read.

Instructional Resources
❏ **All in One Teaching Resources**
  L3 Section Quiz, p. 26
❏ **Reading and Note Taking Study Guide**
(On-Level, Adapted, and Spanish)
Section 3 Summary
❏ **Progress Monitoring Transparencies,** 136

AN ERA OF PROTEST AND CHANGE 1960–1980

4. The Environmental Movement

Pacing
2 periods
1 block

L1	Special Needs
L2	Basic to Average
L3	All Students
L4	Average to Advanced

Section Objectives

■ Assess the causes and effects of the environmental movement.

■ Analyze why environmental protection became a controversial issue.

Terms and People • Rachel Carson • toxic waste • Earth Day • EPA • Clean Air Act • Clean Water Act • Endangered Species Act

Focus Question: What forces gave rise to the environmental movement, and what impact did it have?

PREPARE TO READ

Build Background Knowledge
Preview the section, and remind students that previous President Theodore Roosevelt created national parks because he feared the land would be used for industry.

Set a Purpose
Have students discuss the Witness History Selection. Point out the Section Focus Question, and have students fill in the Note Taking graphic organizer.

Preview Key Terms
Preview the section's Key Terms.

Instructional Resources
❏ **WITNESS HISTORY** Audio CD
❏ **Reading and Note Taking Study Guide**
(On-Level, Adapted, and Spanish)
Section 4

TEACH

Environmental Activists Speak Out
Discuss the factors that led to a rise in environmental awareness and to increased government protection of the environment.

Environmental Setbacks
Describe the events of Love Canal and Three Mile Island as well as growing opposition to environmental regulation.

Instructional Resources
❏ **All in One Teaching Resources**
   L3 Issues Connector: Interaction with the Environment, p. 15
   L3 Reading a Chart: Nuclear Energy, p. 23
❏ **Color Transparencies**
   L3 Three Mile Island, p. 74
❏ **Note Taking Transparencies,** B-141

ASSESS/RETEACH

Assess Progress
Evaluate student comprehension with the Section Assessment and Section Quiz.

Reteach
Assign the Reading and Note Taking Study Guide to help struggling students.

Extend
Extend the lesson by having students complete the online activity on the environment in the 1960s and 1970s.

Instructional Resources
❏ **All in One Teaching Resources**
   L3 Section Quiz, p. 27
   L1 L2 Chapter Test A, p. 28
   L3 Chapter Test B, p. 31
❏ **Reading and Note Taking Study Guide**
(On-Level, Adapted, and Spanish)
Section 4 Summary
❏ **Progress Monitoring Transparencies,** 137

Audio support is available for this section.
Modify lesson with notes found on the bottom of the Teacher's Edition.

Preread the Chapter: Why and How?

What is **Prereading?** It is a reading comprehension strategy. This graphic organizer aids you in prereading this chapter.

Checklist: *Place a check on the line when you have completed the following:*

_____ Read all items in the Chapter Opener.

_____ Read the titles of the charts, graphs, maps, and timeline in the Quick Study Guide and Concept Connector Cumulative Review.

_____ Read the chapter assessment.

Before you read each section of your text, look at the following material. (Chapters may have 3, 4, or 5 sections.) Check the sections as you complete the review.

Sections: 1_____ 2_____ 3_____ 4_____ 5_____ Read the Focus Question, the section opener information in the side column, and each boldface heading and subheading.

Sections: 1_____ 2_____ 3_____ 4_____ 5_____ Looked over all words that are underlined or in boldface type.

Sections: 1_____ 2_____ 3_____ 4_____ 5_____ Read all review questions within the section.

Complete the following:

1. Chapter title: _____

2. Write the main idea of each section based on its Focus Question.

   Section 1: _____

   _____

   Section 2: _____

   _____

   Section 3: _____

   _____

   Section 4: _____

   _____

   Section 5: _____

   _____

Preread the Chapter: Why and How? (Continued)

3. List three visual aids included in the chapter (e.g., pictures, maps, charts, diagrams, features). Describe how they will aid your understanding of the chapter.

   (1) _____

   _____

   (2) _____

   _____

   (3) _____

   _____

4. Describe one new or important idea you learned from reading the Quick Study Guide.

   _____

   _____

5. Identify two unfamiliar words that you noticed during your prereading, and determine from the context what you think the new word means.

   Word #1 _____ Part of Speech _____

   Clues to meaning _____

   Predicted meaning _____

   Word #2 _____ Part of Speech _____

   Clues to meaning _____

   Predicted meaning _____

6. After previewing this chapter, were you able to understand what the chapter is about?

   Not understood _____ Somewhat understood _____ Easily understood _____

7. Copy the heading (titles in blue print) that you predict will be the most difficult to understand.

   _____

   _____

8. How many pages are in the chapter? _____

9. Estimate the time it will take you to read the chapter. _____

Analyze Visuals

Images are an effective way to communicate information. There are many types of visuals, such as photographs, paintings, and Infographics. Visuals tell a story in a dramatic or vivid style. Just as with any primary or secondary source, it is important to look closely and ask questions to determine the meaning and reliability of the visual.

Use this outline to help you better understand ideas or events conveyed by a visual. Answer these questions to the best of your ability.

Title of visual _____ Page _____

1. What is the topic of the visual (what is happening)?

   _____

2. Focus on the details and list three that you find in the visual. How does each help convey information about the topic?

   _____

   _____

   _____

3. Assume you are one of the individuals in the picture, or that you were present when the image was made.

   (a) Describe who you are.

   _____

   (b) Explain what your reaction might have been to the situation.

   _____

   _____

4. The creator often reveals a bias about the subject or an attempt to get a response from the viewer. Is there anything you see in the image that tells the creator's point of view?

   _____

   _____

5. Write your own caption for the image.

   _____

Vocabulary Builder

Make Word Maps

Word maps help you organize different kinds of information about new vocabulary. When you make word maps, you learn and use unfamiliar words in several ways. The example below provides the textbook definition, synonyms, word origins, and related words for the term *contradict*.

Example

Definition *v.* to go against expressed views

Synonyms contravene, deny, negate, refute

contradict

Word origins Latin *contradictus: contra–*, against; *dicere*, to speak

Related words contradiction, contradictory, contradictious

Directions: *On a separate sheet of paper, make a word map for each word listed below. Then, in the space provided write a sentence using each word.*

1. gender _____

_____

_____

2. implement _____

_____

_____

3. compel _____

_____

_____

AN ERA OF PROTEST AND CHANGE

Reading Strategy

Identify Causes and Effects

Every event in history happens as a result of other events. These initial events represent **causes** of the later event, which in turn causes changes of its own. Those changes represent **effects** of the event. Identifying the causes and effects of events will help you understand how different moments in history relate to one another.

Read the following paragraph:

> Second wave feminism rose in the 1960s. The civil rights movement motivated women to explore the discrimination they faced in society. Many women began to demand gender equality in political, social, and legal ways. The women's movement led to many changes including legislation that ensured women's equal treatment, more women participating in the workforce, and greater rights under the law.

In this example, the event is the second wave feminism movement. One cause of this movement is the earlier civil rights movement. The effects of second wave feminism are increased rights for women in a variety of areas.

Directions: *Read the following paragraph. Then, on a separate sheet of paper, answer the questions below.*

> Betty Friedan helped organize the National Organization for Women (NOW) several years after writing *The Feminine Mystique*. She sought to break down discriminatory barriers in the workplace and in education. NOW, along with other groups, filed lawsuits against employers who discriminated against women. Two pieces of legislation that resulted from such lawsuits were Title IX of the Higher Education Act of 1972, which secured equal education for women, and the Equal Credit Opportunity Act in 1974, which made it illegal for companies to deny credit on the basis of gender.

> **Hint:** First, identify the central event. Then, look for reasons it occurred and changes that followed.

1. Identify the central event in this paragraph.

   _____

2. What was one cause of the central event?

   _____

   _____

3. List two effects of the central event.

   _____

   _____

Enrichment: Time Capsule

1969

The 1960s marked a period of social and political upheaval. Musicians such as Bob Dylan and musical groups such as the Fifth Dimension sang songs about social and political change. Richard Nixon was inaugurated 37th president of the United States. Neil Armstrong and Buzz Aldrin walked on the moon. Woodstock provided three days of peace and music, but the Vietnam War continued.

Your assignment: Work in a small group to identify objects for a time capsule depicting 1969 and the baby-boom generation's hope for the future. Then, prepare and present a mock ceremony marking the 1969 burial of the time capsule.

Suggested materials: a cardboard box decorated with images of the 1960s; five items depicting 1969; one item depicting the baby-boom generation's hope for the future; lyrics and audio recordings of two popular songs from the 1960s; audio equipment; costumes for your group to wear from the 1960s; printed programs

Suggested resources: teachers, parents, grandparents, and friends and relatives who grew up in the 1960s; school-approved websites on American cultural history; magazines and newspapers from the 1960s

Suggested procedure:

1. Find a large cardboard box, and decorate it with images from the 1960s. Research art, posters, and other symbols of the time to create your decorations.

2. Use the chart on the next page to identify items that symbolize the 1960s. Choose one item for each of the categories. Also, identify one item you think would symbolize the world that baby-boomers envisioned for their families in 2069. Explain why you chose each item for the time capsule in the chart.

3. Identify two popular songs from the 1960s that you think best depict the era. Find lyrics and audio recordings for these songs.

4. Prepare a script for the mock burial ceremony. Your script should include an opening song, welcome and introductions, a purpose statement, highlights of the 1960s, an explanation of each item chosen for the time capsule, a statement regarding your hopes for the future, closing comments, and a closing song. Your script should give every member of your group an opportunity to speak during the ceremony.

5. Prepare and reproduce a program to distribute to classmates who attend the mock ceremony. Be sure to include the lyrics of songs to be sung during the ceremony. A sample program is presented on the next page.

6. Practice the mock ceremony before you present it to classmates. Make sure your audio equipment works effectively.

Name _____ Class _____ Date _____

Enrichment: Time Capsule

1969

Directions: *Find and record items representing the year 1969 for each category listed in the table below. Then, in the space provided, explain why you chose that item. When you have completed your research and compiled your objects, prepare a script and a program for your mock burial ceremony. Refer to the sample program below.*

	Symbolic Item	Explanation
World Events		
National Events		
Economics		
Science and Technology		
Arts and Entertainment		
Hope for the Future (i.e., what baby-boomers hoped people would achieve by 2069)		

Sample Program

A 1969 Time Capsule Burial Ceremony
May 1, 1969
My Town, My State, U.S.A.

Opening Song
Welcome and Introductions
Purpose of the Ceremony
Highlights of the 1960s
Presentation and Explanation of Items for Burial
Hope for the Future
Burial of the Time Capsule
Closing Comments
Closing Song

Anticipated Date of Exhumation
May 1, 2069

Lyrics for Songs Attached

AN ERA OF PROTEST AND CHANGE

Issues Connector: Interaction with the Environment

People have always used nature's resources to live and work. In the process of living, people have altered the environment. Congress recognized this complex relationship in 1872 when it designated the Yellowstone wilderness area as a national public park to be enjoyed as well as protected. The selected quotations illustrate Americans' continued interaction with the environment and the role science and government might play in balancing economic development and environmental protection.

Theodore Roosevelt and "The New Nationalism" Theodore Roosevelt's love of nature began at an early age. As a child, he collected specimens and kept notebooks on his observations. At Harvard, Roosevelt studied natural history, and after college he joined groups concerned with conservation. Later, Roosevelt's conservation efforts caused him to help lead a movement to protect Yellowstone from commercial development. Roosevelt's presidency was marked by the creation of more than 50 wildlife refuges in the United States. However, he did not direct his efforts toward preservation alone. In 1902, he created the Federal Reclamation Service, which used dams and irrigation to transform millions of acres of land into farmland. In a speech delivered in Kansas on August 31, 1910, Roosevelt expressed his belief that conservation should include using natural resources as well as preserving the environment.

Rachel Carson and *Silent Spring* Born in 1907, Rachel Carson loved to explore nature and to write. Trained as a scientist, she spent her adult life studying and writing about nature. For 15 years, she worked as a scientist, a writer, and an editor for the federal government. She resigned in 1952 to dedicate more time to writing. Carson questioned the use of chemical pesticides as early as 1945, but publishers refused to publish articles about her concerns. In 1958, her concerns about chemical pesticides grew when a friend expressed suspicions that the DDT used on Cape Cod to kill mosquitoes was also killing birds. Carson's investigations into the dangers of chemical pesticides, especially DDT, prompted her to write *Silent Spring*. In her book, she describes how DDT enters the food chain, settles into body tissue, and causes genetic damage and disease. Initially published in the *New Yorker* as a three-part series in June 1962, *Silent Spring* generated both concern and controversy. Appearing before Congress in 1963, Carson recommended the adoption of policies to protect human health and the environment.

John M. Lee on Reactions to *Silent Spring* Rachel Carson's book drew criticism even before its official release in September 1962. Reporter John M. Lee described the growing controversy in a July 1962 article in the *New York Times*. Lee reported that pesticide manufacturers were already closely reviewing Carson's text, preparing rebuttals, and planning ways to discredit the book. Industry representatives expressed disappointment that Carson failed to acknowledge the benefits of chemical pesticides. They claimed she could have performed a greater public service if she had used her book to describe the benefits of pesticides as well as the need to use them cautiously. Lee said that they resented Carson's implications that the industry was blind to both the potential dangers of pesticides and the need to establish safeguards to prevent their misuse. Some pesticide manufacturers even complained that certain medicines and forms of sanitation posed greater threats to health and the environment. Lee anticipated that *Silent Spring* would generate controversy and debate for many years.

Issues Connector: Interaction with the Environment

Endangered Species Act of 1973 Banned by the federal government in 1972, DDT is just one of many factors that threaten wildlife. President Nixon signed the Endangered Species Act of 1973 to require the federal government to study the impact of human projects on wildlife habitats. The act also forbids people from trading in endangered species or their products. Although limited funding makes the law difficult to enforce, it has been effective in helping stabilize or increase the populations of several species, including the bald eagle.

Kyoto Protocol Initiated in 1997 during a United Nations conference on climate change, the Kyoto Protocol represents an international effort to reduce greenhouse gas emissions believed to cause global warming. Greenhouse gases—such as carbon dioxide, nitrous oxide, methane, and water vapor—exist naturally in the atmosphere and trap heat radiated from Earth, keeping atmospheric temperatures at habitable levels. Pollution from factories and automobiles adds more greenhouse gases to the natural mix, trapping more radiated heat and causing global warming. Polar ice caps melt as global temperatures rise, leading to elevated sea levels and flooding. Other effects include disruptions to agricultural industries, lost habitats leading to the extinction of species, and an increased frequency of tropical storms and tropical diseases. By setting goals and outlining strategies, the 125 nations that have ratified the Kyoto Protocol hope to stop global warming. The United States, which emits about one-fourth of the greenhouse gases that enter the atmosphere, refuses to participate in this international treaty.

George Bush's Position on the Kyoto Protocol Elected to office in 2000, President Bush insisted that the Kyoto Protocol would put the United States at an unfair disadvantage. In a 2001 letter to Senators Hagel, Helms, Craig, and Roberts, Bush explained that participation in the protocol would create economic hardships on business and industry as well as on consumers. He expressed an unwillingness to risk participation when scientists had yet to agree on the nature of global warning and the best strategies to prevent it. He observed that the Senate, in a vote of 95-0, agreed that participation in the protocol was not in the best interests of the United States. However, he did indicate that the United States was taking steps to study the problem and identify solutions that would be in the best interests of the nation, its citizens, and the global community.

AN ERA OF PROTEST AND CHANGE

Issues Connector: Interaction with the Environment

"I recognize the right and duty of this generation to develop and use the natural resources of our land; but I do not recognize the right to waste them, or to rob, by wasteful use, the generations that come after us."

— *Theodore Roosevelt,*
"The New Nationalism," 1910

Only within the moment of time represented by the present century has one species—man—acquired significant power to alter the nature of his world.

— *Rachel Carson,*
Silent Spring, *1962*

Interaction with the Environment

The $300,000,000 pesticides industry has been highly irritated by a quiet woman author whose previous works on science have been praised for the beauty and precision of the writing.... [M]ost say that they can find little error of fact. What they do criticize, however, are the extensions and implications that she gives to isolated case histories of the [negative] effects of certain pesticides used or misused in certain instances. The industry feels that she has presented a one-sided case....

— *John M. Lee,* New York Times,
July 22, 1962

Nothing is more priceless and more worthy of preservation than the rich array of animal life with which our country has been blessed . . .

— *Richard Nixon, Statement made*
on signing the Endangered Species
Act, San Clemente, California,
December 28, 1973

The [participating nations] . . . shall, individually or jointly, ensure that their . . . emissions of the greenhouse gases . . . do not exceed their assigned amounts, calculated [according] to their quantified emission limitation and reduction commitments . . . with a view to reducing their overall emissions of such gases by at least 5 per cent below 1990 levels in the commitment period 2008 to 2012.

— *Article 3, Item 1 of the Kyoto*
Protocol, December 11, 1997

As you know, I oppose the Kyoto Protocol because it exempts 80 percent of the world, including major population centers such as China and India, from compliance, and would cause serious harm to the U.S. economy.... [W]e must be very careful not to take actions that could harm consumers. This is especially true given the incomplete state of scientific knowledge of the causes of, and solutions to, global climate change . . .

— *George Bush, excerpt from letter,*
March 13, 2001

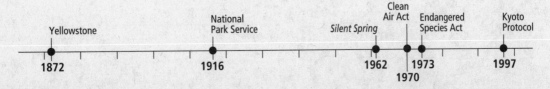

Name _____ Class _____ Date _____

Issues Connector: Interaction with the Environment

Directions: *Read the excerpts regarding the issue of Interaction with the Environment, and answer the following questions.*

1. According to Rachel Carson, what role do humans play in the environment?

   _____

   _____

2. What does John Lee say is the pesticide industry's response to *Silent Spring*?

   _____

   _____

3. How much importance does President Nixon give the Endangered Species Act of 1973? Explain your answer.

   _____

   _____

4. What is the purpose of the Kyoto Protocol?

   _____

   _____

5. What stand does President Bush take on the Kyoto Protocol?

   _____

   _____

6. **Draw Conclusions** How might Theodore Roosevelt have reacted to the Endangered Species Act of 1973?

   _____

   _____

7. **Apply Information** Should all high school students be required to ride buses to school or to walk in an effort to reduce greenhouse gas emissions? Explain your position.

   _____

   _____

   _____

AN ERA OF PROTEST AND CHANGE

Link to Literature

Arlo Guthrie (born 1947) helped shape the social consciousness of the counterculture generation through his singing and songwriting. He wrote "Alice's Restaurant" to protest the Vietnam War. Released in 1967, the lengthy song tells a story about Guthrie's decision to help his friend Alice get rid of trash. His decision leads to his arrest for littering and a confrontation with the draft board. As the story goes, the draft board looks at his arrest for littering and questions his moral fitness for military service. Guthrie, in turn, questions the logic of sending morally-fit men into war to kill people. He's quickly labeled a troublemaker and fingerprinted. ◆ *As you read, think about how a writer's words can move a generation of people to action. Then, on a separate sheet of paper, answer the questions that follow.*

"Alice's Restaurant" by Arlo Guthrie

And friends, somewhere in Washington enshrined in some little folder, is a study in black and white of my fingerprints. And the only reason I'm singing you this song now is cause you may know somebody in a similar situation, or you may be in a similar situation, and if [you're] in a situation like that there's only one thing you can do and that's walk into the shrink wherever you are, just walk in say, "Shrink, You can get anything you want, at Alice's restaurant." And walk out. You know, if one person, just one person does it they may think he's really sick and they won't take him. . . .

Arlo Guthrie, ©Bettmann/CORBIS

And if three people do it, three, can you imagine, three people walking in singin a bar of Alice's Restaurant and walking out. They may think it's an organization. And can you, can you imagine fifty people a day, I said fifty people a day walking in singin a bar of Alice's Restaurant and walking out. And friends they may think it's a movement.

And that's what it is, the Alice's Restaurant Anti-Massacre Movement, and all you got to do to join is sing it the next time it [comes] around on the guitar.

Questions to Think About

1. What does Guthrie think will happen when different numbers of people sing his refrain about Alice's restaurant?

2. When does Guthrie say that an idea becomes a movement?

3. **Draw Conclusions** How much of a difference do you think protest songs made in stopping the Vietnam War? Do you think music today has a similar impact on people?

Biography

Gloria Steinem played an important role in the women's rights movement of the 1960s. She wrote articles and books promoting women's rights. She also helped found a feminist magazine called *Ms.* ◆ *Read the following biography. As you read, think about the ways in which Gloria Steinem helped the women's rights movement. Then, on a separate sheet of paper, answer the questions that follow.*

Gloria Steinem (born 1934)

Gloria Steinem loved to write. She was born in 1934 and after graduating from college, she spent two years in India. She came back to the United States and worked as a journalist. However, she didn't often get to report about serious news like her male colleagues did. She also didn't get paid as well. She believed that she just wasn't quite as good as the male reporters.

Steinem's opinion about her reporting skills changed when she attended her first feminist meeting in 1968. At this meeting she heard women talking about the different ways that they had been abused, used, or dismissed. Steinem began to realize that her problems had less to do with her skills and more to do with the way society looks at women. At that point, she decided to use her skills to promote the women's rights movement.

Steinem's first feminist news story appeared in *New York Magazine* in 1969. Entitled "After Black Power, Women's Liberation," it was one of the first stories about the women's movement to appear in a mainstream newspaper. Steinem won an important award for this story. She began

Gloria Steinem,
Library of Congress

to look for other opportunities to report similar stories. Because male editors did not take this kind of news story seriously, she decided the women's movement needed a publication of its own. In the early 1970s, Steinem helped found *Ms.* magazine.

In addition to writing feminist news articles, Steinem wrote books that encouraged people to think about important issues facing women. She also toured the nation, working with other women to give lectures and lead discussions about women's rights. Giving lectures challenged Steinem because public speaking frightened her. With practice, she overcame her fears and developed strong public speaking skills.

Steinem also worked with organizations to help women. In 1971, she helped found the National Women's Political Caucus and the Women's Action Alliance. In 1977, she helped plan the National Women's Conference in Houston, Texas. Steinem used her skills to generate awareness about women's issues and helped foster a shift in attitudes about roles and opportunities for women.

Questions to Think About

1. List five ways that Gloria Steinem helped promote the women's movement.

2. What skills did Gloria Steinem bring to the women's movement? What skills did she develop in her work with the movement?

3. **Recognize Cause and Effect** Why do you think Gloria Steinem joined the women's movement?

AN ERA OF PROTEST AND CHANGE

Biography

Women's Rights Activists

Elizabeth Cady Stanton, Gloria Steinem, and Shirley Chisholm played prominent roles in the women's movement that began in 1848. Their willingness to overcome obstacles and pay the price of participation helped generate awareness of women's rights as well as legislative action. ◆ *Read the following biographies. As you read, think about the experiences that motivated these activists. Then, on a separate sheet of paper, answer the questions that follow.*

Elizabeth Cady Stanton (1815–1902) believed women should be full participants in society. In 1840, she attended an international anti-slavery convention, but event organizers banned Stanton and other female delegates from the convention floor. Eight years later, she and four other women planned the first women's rights convention. Stanton helped organize and drive the women's suffrage movement despite her husband's opposition. She also advocated coeducation, liberal divorce laws, and dress reform. Stanton toured the nation promoting her views until she died in 1902.

Elizabeth Cady Stanton,
Library of Congress

As a journalist, Gloria Steinem (born 1934) had trouble getting serious reporting assignments and earning wages comparable to male reporters. She assumed she just wasn't good enough until she attended her first feminist meeting in 1968. After hearing stories about other women's experiences, Steinem concluded that society systematically discriminated against women. She decided to use her writing skills to advance the feminist movement. Her first feminist article appeared in 1969 in *New York Magazine.* Because male-dominated news establishments did not support her reporting interests, Steinem helped found *Ms.* magazine in the early 1970s so she could continue to report on the women's movement.

Gloria Steinem,
Library of Congress

As an educator, Shirley Chisholm (1924–2005) observed daily the effects of poverty. These observations led her to run for the New York State legislature, where she served from 1964 to 1968. In 1968, Chisholm became the first African American woman elected to Congress. She considered the distinction foolish because it reflected the views of a society that was neither just nor free. From 1969 to 1983, she served in the House of Representatives, where she advocated for the poor, opposed the Vietnam War, and supported women's rights. In 1972, she competed for the Democratic nomination for president.

Shirley Chisholm,
Library of Congress

Questions to Think About

1. What examples of discrimination did Stanton and Steinem experience?

2. Why did Gloria Steinem help found *Ms.* magazine?

3. **Draw Conclusions** How successful do you believe Stanton, Steinem, and Chisholm were in achieving their goals? Explain your answer.

Name _____ Class _____ Date _____

Because migrant workers traveled from state to state, they were among the most exploited workers in the nation in the 1960s. The United Farm Workers organized to improve wages and working conditions for migrant farmworkers in the 1960s and 1970s. ◆ *Reread the paragraphs under the heading "Cesar Chavez Organizes Farmworkers" in Section 3 of your textbook. Then, provide a caption for what you see in each frame of the cartoon strip below. When you finish, answer the question at the bottom of the page.*

Cesar Chavez and the UFW

_____ _____

_____ _____

_____

_____

Chris Vallo

_____ _____

_____ _____

Critical Thinking Explain why you think the unions were important to migrant farmworkers.

Name _____ Class _____ Date _____

Reading a Chart

In the 1970s, nuclear energy promised a clean alternative to the use of fossil fuels. Some people argued that nuclear energy produces less harmful emissions than burning fossil fuels, and is therefore good for the environment. However, the nuclear malfunction at Three Mile Island frightened Americans. Although the accident posed no health risks, many wondered if the benefits of nuclear energy truly outweighed its potential costs. These people argued that harmful toxic waste is too dangerous to handle safely. Many years later, Americans still debate the use of nuclear energy. ◆ *Read the chart below and the section under the heading "Environmental Setbacks" in Section 4 of your textbook. Then, answer the questions on a separate sheet of paper.*

Nuclear Energy

Nuclear Energy	
Advantages	Disadvantages
• Nuclear power plants are less expensive to operate than plants powered by fossil fuels. • Nuclear power plants require smaller amounts of fuel to operate. • Nuclear power plants do not pollute the air with chemical gases or solid particles.	• Nuclear power plants are more expensive to build than plants powered by fossil fuels. • Accidents may contaminate with radioactivity areas inside and outside the plants. • Nuclear waste products require careful disposal because they remain highly radioactive for long periods of time.

Questions to Think About

1. What do you think is the most important advantage of nuclear energy? Explain your answer.

2. What do you think is the most important disadvantage of nuclear energy? Explain your answer.

3. **Apply Information** Knowing what you have learned about the pros and cons of nuclear energy, do you believe that the United States should continue to use nuclear energy? Explain your answer.

Name _____ Class _____ Date _____

Section 1 Quiz

A. Key Terms and People

Directions: *From Column II below, choose the person or term that best fits each description.*

Column I

_____ 1. former researcher who encouraged drug use

_____ 2. small community of people who share resources

_____ 3. San Francisco district popular with the counterculture

_____ 4. lack of communication between adults and youth

_____ 5. group of people rebelling against tradition in the 1960s

_____ 6. a popular English rock band in the 1960s

Column II

a. counterculture

b. generation gap

c. Beatles

d. commune

e. Haight-Ashbury

f. Timothy Leary

B. Key Concepts

Directions: *Write the letter of the best answer or ending in each blank.*

_____ 7. Which event helped create the counterculture of the 1960s and 1970s?

    a. Great Depression   c. Vietnam War

    b. World War II   d. Woodstock

_____ 8. One interest that defined the counterculture was

    a. classical music.   c. university courses.

    b. self-centered ideals.   d. Eastern spirituality.

_____ 9. Why did the music and clothing industries market products for the counterculture?

    a. People refused to buy anything similar to their parents' clothes.

    b. Members of the counterculture represented a large consumer group.

    c. Countercultural music and clothing appealed to everyone.

    d. Members of the counterculture managed these industries.

_____ 10. Which defining characteristic of the counterculture provided the foundation for the various rights movements that followed it?

    a. protest   c. communes

    b. drug use   d. youthfulness

AN ERA OF PROTEST AND CHANGE

Section 2 Quiz

A. Key Terms and People

Directions: *Read each sentence, decide whether it is true or false, and then mark T or F in the blank to the left of the number. If the sentence is false, rewrite the underlined portion so that it is correct.*

_____ 1. The proposed amendment to the U.S. Constitution, called <u>NOW</u>, would guarantee equal rights for women.

_____ 2. *The Feminine Mystique,* written by <u>Gloria Steinem</u>, questioned the limited roles for women in society.

_____ 3. <u>Phyllis Schlafly</u> worked to defeat an equal rights amendment for women.

_____ 4. <u>Feminism</u> holds that men and women are equal politically, socially, and economically.

_____ 5. <u>*Roe* v. *Wade*</u> protected a woman's right to have an abortion.

_____ 6. <u>Betty Friedan</u>, cofounder of *Ms.* Magazine, worked to raise awareness of women's right through the mass media.

B. Key Concepts

Directions: *Write the letter of the best answer or ending in each blank.*

_____ 7. The National Organization for Women focused in part on
 a. defeating the ERA.
 b. reforming the existing political system.
 c. protecting reproductive freedom.
 d. discouraging marriage.

_____ 8. The Equal Credit Opportunity Act of 1974 made it illegal to deny credit to someone because of
 a. gender.   c. marital status.
 b. race.   d. sexual orientation.

_____ 9. The women's movement caused
 a. the number of married female workers to decrease.
 b. the number of women in the workforce to double from 1950 to 2000.
 c. women's wages to rise to match men's wages.
 d. workers of the world to demand equal treatment.

_____ 10. The "pink collar ghetto" refers to the
 a. wage disparity between men and women.
 b. women's rights movement.
 c. class of women business leaders.
 d. women who opposed the equal rights amendment.

AN ERA OF PROTEST AND CHANGE

Section 3 Quiz

A. Key Terms and People

Directions: *Choose the person or term that best completes each sentence.*

Column I

_____ 1. _____ move from place to place in search of work.

_____ 2. The _____ worked to increase Latino awareness of their history and culture.

_____ 3. Chippewa activists founded _____ to help Native Americans secure their legal rights.

_____ 4. _____ worked to protect consumers from harmful products and unethical business practices.

_____ 5. _____ organized a farm workers' union to help protect exploited workers.

_____ 6. The _____ implemented a workers' strike and consumer boycott of table grapes in the late 1960s.

Column II

a. Cesar Chavez

b. UFW

c. migrant farmworkers

d. Chicano movement

e. AIM

f. Ralph Nader

B. Key Concepts

Directions: *Write the letter of the best answer or ending in each blank.*

_____ 7. Which factor contributed to a rise in Latin American immigration in the mid-1900s?

    a. slow population growth in Latin America

    b. the collapse of dictatorships in Latin America

    c. the end of the *bracero* program in the United States

    d. a growing demand for cheap labor in the United States

_____ 8. In 1969, American Indians occupied Alcatraz primarily to

    a. establish a new nation.   **c.** protest prison policies.

    b. celebrate their culture.   **d.** call attention to broken treaties.

_____ 9. Consumer advocacy efforts resulted in

    a. more workplace safety regulations.

    b. greater automaker control over car production.

    c. less government oversight of industry.

    d. lower prices on consumer goods.

_____ 10. Which of the following directly benefited people with disabilities?

    a. the Pure Food and Drug Act   **c.** the Special Olympics

    b. *Unsafe at Any Speed*   **d.** the "long march" to Washington, D.C.

AN ERA OF PROTEST AND CHANGE

Section 4 Quiz

A. Reviewing Key Terms

Directions: *From Column II below, choose the term that best fits each description. You will not use all of the answers.*

Column I

_____ 1. law protecting animals and plants in danger of extinction

_____ 2. law requiring that factories and cars reduce their toxic emissions

_____ 3. government agency created to protect the environment

_____ 4. poisonous byproducts of human activity

_____ 5. law requiring factories and farms to reduce water pollution

_____ 6. a nationwide protest meant to raise awareness of environmental concerns

Column II

a. Rachel Carson

b. toxic waste

c. Earth Day

d. EPA

e. Clean Air Act

f. Clean Water Act

g. Endangered Species Act

B. Key Concepts

Directions: *Write the letter of the best answer or ending in each blank.*

_____ 7. Congress responded to the 1962 publication of Rachel Carson's *Silent Spring* by
   a. restricting the use of DDT.
   b. enacting Earth Day.
   c. funding the Love Canal cleanup.
   d. promoting the Sierra Club's efforts.

_____ 8. Which President encouraged Congress to create the EPA and signed a number of environmental laws?
   a. John F. Kennedy
   b. Lyndon Johnson
   c. Richard Nixon
   d. Gerald Ford

_____ 9. The Love Canal contamination and other events involving hazardous waste prompted Congress to
   a. establish Superfund.
   b. set up the Nuclear Regulatory Commission.
   c. take state control of industry.
   d. revoke the EPA's oversight authority.

_____ 10. Some conservatives opposed environmental regulations because they worried that the laws would
   a. hamper business.
   b. create too many new jobs.
   c. limit federal authority.
   d. give property owners too much control.

AN ERA OF PROTEST AND CHANGE

Test A

A. Key Terms and People

Directions: *Choose the person or term that best completes each sentence. (3 points each)*

Column I

_____ 1. Farm workers set up a union called the _____.

_____ 2. _____ celebrations remind people to protect the environment.

_____ 3. Many baby boomers listened to the _____ on their radios.

_____ 4. _____ dedicated itself to true equality for women.

_____ 5. _____ helped Latino farm workers.

_____ 6. _____ made abortion legal.

_____ 7. Members of the _____ rebelled against their parents.

_____ 8. _____ is a poisonous by-product of human activity.

_____ 9. _____ asserts that men and woman are equal.

_____ 10. _____ called attention to the dangers of pesticides.

Column II

a. counterculture
b. feminism
c. Beatles
d. *Roe* v. *Wade*
e. Rachel Carlson
f. UFW
g. toxic waste
h. Cesar Chavez
i. NOW
j. Earth Day

B. Key Concepts

Directions: *Write the letter of the best answer or ending in each blank. (4 points each)*

_____ 11. Why was the baby boom generation hard to ignore?
　　a. There were so many of them.
　　b. They were pleasant and attractive.
　　c. Most older Americans died in World War II.

_____ 12. The sexual revolution of the 1960s and 1970s encouraged people to
　　a. get married as teenagers.　　c. talk openly about sex.
　　b. avoid sexual behavior.

_____ 13. Unlike feminists of the past, second-wave feminists wanted to
　　a. register for military draft.　　c. reject marriage and family.
　　b. achieve full equality with men.

Directions: *Use the chart below to answer questions 14 and 15.*

Civilian Labor Force Participation Rates for Women, 1950 to 2000 and projected to 2010 (in percent)							
Age Group	1950	1960	1970	1980	1990	2000	2010
16–24	43.9	42.8	51.3	61.9	63.1	63.2	65.1
25–34	34.0	36.0	45.0	65.5	73.6	76.3	81.4
35–44	39.1	43.4	51.1	65.5	76.5	77.3	80.0
45–54	37.9	49.9	54.4	59.9	71.2	76.8	80.0
55–64	27.0	37.2	43.0	41.3	45.3	51.8	55.2
65 and older	9.7	10.8	9.7	8.1	8.7	9.4	11.1

Source: Monthly Labor Review, May 2002

_____ 14. Between 1970 and 1980, women between the ages of _____ showed the greatest increase in employment.

    a. 16 and 24   **b.** 25 and 34   **c.** 35 and 44

_____ 15. Which of the following probably explains why women have increasingly joined the workforce?

    a. Women have more opportunities.

    b. Fewer men are competing for jobs.

    c. Laws restrict male employment.

_____ 16. How did the U.S. government increase Mexican immigration?

    a. Congress passed laws admitting all Latinos fleeing dictators.

    b. The president ordered the use of collective bargaining.

    c. The *bracero* program granted temporary guest worker status.

_____ 17. What did Native Americans do to call attention to their needs?

    a. formed groups such as AIM to address civil rights issues

    b. took control of all federal prisons on Native American land

    c. led a national boycott of California grapes

_____ 18. How did life change for people with disabilities in the 1960s and 1970s?

    a. The president started an athletic camp called the Special Olympics.

    b. Congress passed several laws granting them equal access to education.

    c. The media encouraged them to hide their disabilities.

Name _____ Class _____ Date _____

_____ 19. The environmental movement began when
   a. counterculture groups held Earth Day activities.
   b. Congress created the Environmental Protection Agency.
   c. coal smog, pesticide abuse, and polluted rivers drew media attention.

_____ 20. Environmental problems led Americans to disagree about whether the government should
   a. declare Earth Day a national holiday.
   b. set up national parks in major cities.
   c. regulate the use of private property.

C.   Document-Based Assessment

Directions: *Use the quotation below to answer question 21 on a separate sheet of paper. (10 points)*

> We have been too . . . willing to leave it to others to clean up our environment. . . . Each of us must resolve that each day he will leave his home, his property, the public places of the city or town a little cleaner, a little better, a little more pleasant for himself and those around him.
>
> —*Richard Nixon, State of the Union Address, January 22, 1970*

21. According to this quotation, how did Nixon want to protect the environment?

D.   Critical Thinking

Directions: *Answer the following questions on a separate sheet of paper. (10 points each)*

22. Compare and Contrast Describe the values of the counterculture. How were these values similar to previous movements, such as the Beat and civil rights movements? How were these values different from those of previous generations?

23. Link Past and Present What changes resulted from the second wave of feminism? Were these changes positive or negative? Explain your answer.

Test B

A. Key Terms and People

Directions: *Match each term in Column II with the number of the correct definition from Column I. You will not use all of the answers. (2 points each)*

Column I

_____ 1. union for Latino and Filipino farmworkers

_____ 2. event promoting environmental protection

_____ 3. English rock band

_____ 4. organization advocating women's rights

_____ 5. Latino union leader

_____ 6. 1973 Supreme Court case on abortion rights

_____ 7. 1960s lifestyle challenging traditional mainstream values

_____ 8. poisonous byproduct of human activity

_____ 9. theory of full equality between men and women

_____ 10. political radical who encouraged people to reject mainstream society

Column II

a. commune

b. counterculture

c. Timothy Leary

d. feminism

e. Beatles

f. Phyllis Schlafly

g. *Roe* v. *Wade*

h. migrant farmworkers

i. Betty Friedan

j. UFW

k. toxic waste

l. Cesar Chavez

m. NOW

n. Earth Day

B. Key Concepts

Directions: *Write the letter of the best answer or ending in each blank. (4 points each)*

_____ 11. What did the baby boom generation value?

    a. traditional, mainstream values

    b. trust in adults and the government

    c. youth, spontaneity, individuality, and spirituality

    d. restriction on minority civil rights and environmental regulation

_____ 12. How did the sexual revolution of the 1960s and 1970s affect society?

    a. Teenage marriages increased.

    b. Sexually transmitted diseases declined.

    c. Individuals talked openly about sex.

    d. Divorce rates decreased.

_____ 13. The second wave of feminism differed from the first wave because modern women wanted

    a. full equality with men, not just the right to vote.

    b. superiority over the men in their lives.

    c. voting rights.

    d. a return to more traditional roles.

Name _____ Class _____ Date _____

Directions: *Use the chart below to answer questions 14 and 15.*

Civilian Labor Force Participation Rates for Women, 1950 to 2000 and projected to 2010 (in percent)							
Age Group	1950	1960	1970	1980	1990	2000	2010
16–24	43.9	42.8	51.3	61.9	63.1	63.2	65.1
25–34	34.0	36.0	45.0	65.5	73.6	76.3	81.4
35–44	39.1	43.4	51.1	65.5	76.5	77.3	80.0
45–54	37.9	49.9	54.4	59.9	71.2	76.8	80.0
55–64	27.0	37.2	43.0	41.3	45.3	51.8	55.2
65 and older	9.7	10.8	9.7	8.1	8.7	9.4	11.1

Source: Monthly Labor Review, May 2002

_____ 14. Which age group of women showed the greatest percentage increase in labor force participation between 1950 and 2000?

a. 16–24   c. 35–44

b. 25–34   d. 45–54

_____ 15. Which of the following factors explains the general pattern in women's participation in the labor force?

a. As women's roles have expanded, more women have entered the workforce.

b. As opposition to women's rights has increased, fewer women have joined the workforce.

c. As baby boomers age, fewer people are working past age 65.

d. The women's rights movement has led to fewer women taking low-paying jobs.

_____ 16. The Chicano movement

a. focused on migrant workers' rights.

b. led people to boycott California grapes.

c. encouraged Latinos to form self-governing reservations.

d. increased Latinos' awareness of their history and culture.

_____ 17. The American Indian Movement confronted the government through

a. protests for the preservation of native fishing rights.

b. a march from San Francisco to Washington, D.C.

c. a political party that sought to win seats in Congress.

d. programs designed to decrease unemployment and other social ills.

_____ 18. People with disabilities gained expanded civil rights through
    a. people's recognition of FDR's disability.
    b. Ralph Nader's book and lobbying efforts.
    c. laws that guaranteed them equal access to education.
    d. a constitutional amendment prohibiting discrimination based on disability.

_____ 19. The catastrophe at Three Mile Island pointed out the hazards of
    a. coal smog   **c.** acid rain
    b. nuclear reactors   **d.** pesticides

_____ 20. Congress established Superfund to
    a. clean up toxic wastes.
    b. regulate nuclear energy plants.
    c. protect endangered plants and animals.
    d. find alternative sources of energy to coal and oil.

C. Document-Based Assessment

Directions: *Use the quotation below to answer question 21 on a separate sheet of paper.*
(10 points)

> We still think of air as free. But clean air is not free, and neither is clean water. The price tag on pollution control is high. Through our years of past carelessness we incurred [gained] a debt to nature, and now that debt is being called. . . . Now, I realize that the argument is often made that there is a fundamental contradiction between economic growth and the quality of life, so that to have one we must forsake the other. The answer is not to abandon growth, but to redirect it. For example, we should turn toward ending congestion and eliminating smog the same reservoir of inventive genius that created them in the first place.
>
> —*Richard Nixon, State of the Union Address, January 22, 1970*

21. Explain how this quotation demonstrates Nixon's role as an environmental president.

D. Critical Thinking

Directions: *Answer the following questions on a separate sheet of paper. (10 points each)*

22. Link Past and Present Did the second wave of feminism succeed in establishing equality for women? Explain your answer.

23. Draw Inferences What events influenced the growth of the environmental movement in the United States? Explain whether the environmental movement has had a positive or negative effect on the United States.

Answer Key

Vocabulary Builder

Students' responses should demonstrate understanding of the vocabulary.

Reading Strategy

1. Betty Friedan organizes NOW.
2. Women were experiencing discrimination in education and in the workplace.
3. Congress passed Title IX of the Higher Education Act of 1972, which secured equal education for women, and the Equal Credit Opportunity Act in 1974, which made it illegal for companies to deny credit on the basis of gender.

Enrichment

Students' projects should demonstrate research, creative thinking, and appropriate presentation. Use *Assessment Rubrics* to evaluate the project.

Issues Connector
Interaction with the Environment

1. Rachel Carson believes that humans, by their capacity to make conscious choices, have the power to both damage and protect the environment.
2. John Lee says that Rachel Carson selectively used facts to give a one-sided view of pesticides.
3. Nixon appears to give endangered species legislation great importance. He describes wildlife as a priceless blessing that must be preserved and is worth preserving.
4. The purpose of the Kyoto Protocol is to reduce greenhouse gas emissions to levels that are 5% below the levels for 1990 and to do this by 2012.
5. President Bush says that participation in the Kyoto Protocol would cause economic hardships and that he is unwilling to participate until scientists agree on the causes of and solutions to global warming.

6. Possible response: Roosevelt would have approved of the act because he loved nature and worked during his own presidency to protect wild areas. In his statement, he says that humans have an obligation to protect the land.
7. Students should state an opinion and explain their position.

Link to Literature
"Alice's Restaurant"

1. One person singing the refrain will avoid the draft because he will be considered sick. Three people will give the impression that an organization is behind them. Fifty people singing the refrain will look like a movement and will make the authorities pay attention.
2. An idea becomes a movement when vast numbers of people speak with one voice.
3. Possible response: Protest songs helped communicate the antiwar message and encouraged people to join together to push for peace. Students may say that music has a strong impact and can be a force for change. Other students may say that music is aimed toward making profits and not toward urging social change.

Biography
Gloria Steinem

1. Possible responses: wrote news stories, founded *Ms.* magazine, wrote feminist articles, wrote books about women's issues, gave lectures about women's rights, helped start the National Women's Political Caucus and Women's Action Alliance, helped plan the National Women's Conference
2. Gloria Steinem brought her reporting and writing skills to the women's movement. As she toured the nation giving lectures, she developed her public speaking skills.
3. Possible response: Steinem joined the women's movement because she had

experienced discrimination and she had heard that other women were experiencing discrimination.

Biography
Women's Rights Activists

1. Stanton was excluded from conventions and from voting. Steinem experienced discrimination in her workplace.
2. Gloria Steinem helped found *Ms.* magazine because she believed that the women's movement needed a publication of its own so it did not have to compete for space in male-dominated publications that did not take the women's movement seriously.
3. Possible responses: If success is defined as having one's voice heard, then all three women were successful. Women attended the first women's rights conference in 1848, and people listened to Stanton's lectures. Many people bought and read Steinem's *Ms.* magazine. People elected Chisholm as their representative in Washington. If success is defined as eliminating discrimination against women, then the success of these three women would have to be described as partial. Advances have been made, but the struggle for full equality continues.

History Comics
Cesar Chavez and the UFW

Ceasar Chavez organizes a union for Latino farm laborers in Delano, California. / The Latino farm laborer organization joins the Filipino organization to become the United Farm Workers. They strike for better pay and conditions. / The strike gets the attention of U.S. citizens who join the protest. / Consumers support the boycott by refusing to buy grapes. / The strike and boycott hurt the grape growers, but the government responds to the concern for workers' rights. / California passes a law in 1975 requiring collective bargaining between growers and union

representatives. / Migrant farmworkers were often fired if they complained about conditions or tried to unionize. These unions finally allowed an exploited group of workers to settle issues and fight the deplorable conditions of their work.

Reading a Chart
Nuclear Energy

1. Students should identify an advantage and explain their reasoning.
2. Students should identify a disadvantage and explain their reasoning.
3. Students may say that the United States should use nuclear energy because it is a cheap, clean way to get power that has caused few problems in the United States when handled properly. Other students may say that the United States should abandon nuclear power because its benefits do not outweigh the risks.

Section 1 Quiz

1. f	2. d	3. e	4. b	5. a
6. c	7. c	8. d	9. b	10. a

Section 2 Quiz

1. F, ERA
2. F, Betty Friedan
3. T
4. T
5. T
6. F, Gloria Steinem
7. c   8. a   9. b   10. a

Section 3 Quiz

1. f	2. d	3. e	4. f	5. a
6. b	7. d	8. d	9. a	10. c

Section 4 Quiz

1. g	2. e	3. d	4. b	5. f
6. c	7. a	8. c	9. a	10. a

Answer Key

Test A

1. f	2. j	3. c	4. i	5. h
6. c	7. a	8. g	9. b	10. a
11. a	12. c	13. b	14. b	15. a
16. c	17. a	18. b	19. c	20. c

21. In this quotation, Nixon wanted all Americans to protect the environment by keeping their homes and public places cleaner and more pleasant.

22. Like the Beat movement, the counter-culture valued freedom from materialism and stressed the importance of personal experience. The counterculture also questioned boundaries and restrictions as the earlier civil rights movement had. The counterculture valued youth and spontaneity, unlike their parents' generation, which valued loyalty and conformity. The antiwar aspect of the counterculture distrusted government and encouraged protest. The previous generation emphasized respect for government authority.

23. The second wave of feminism used the Civil Rights Act of 1964 to challenge discrimination. NOW and other groups compelled the government to enforce the act to reduce discrimination. Title IX of the Higher Education Act of 1972 banned discrimination in education. The Equal Credit Opportunity Act made it illegal to deny credit based on gender. The movement led the Supreme Court to uphold women's right to legal abortions, and led to women's increased presence in the workforce. Students should explain whether they consider these changes positive or negative.

Test B

1. j	2. n	3. e	4. m	5. l
6. g	7. b	8. k	9. d	10. h
11. c	12. c	13. a	14. b	15. a
16. d	17. b	18. c	19. c	20. a

21. In this quotation, Nixon recognizes that economic growth caused environmental problems, and that it is time to fix those problems. He suggests that the people who helped the nation achieve industrial strength should now focus on solving environmental problems. Nixon says that this means redirecting not stopping economic development. For example, perhaps more jobs could be created to address problems. These points demonstrate Nixon's commitment to environmental issues.

22. Students may say that the movement succeeded, because women now have more opportunities. Professions once closed to women, such as medicine, law, and accounting, are now open, and many women face less discrimination on a daily basis. Students may also say that women now have more control over their reproductive health. Students may also say that the movement failed because many women now live below the poverty line. Since the poor are increasingly single women, the changes may have created new problems rather than ending discrimination. Students may suggest that women still suffer from economic and social discrimination.

23. Environmental problems drew attention because of events like the London coal smog and the meltdown at Three Mile Island. Books such as *Silent Spring* pointed out that environmental problems affect the quality of life for many different people.

CURRICULUM